tea
two sugars

by gemma lynch

For my dad.
Always, always for you.

For my family and friends.
Thank you for wholeheartedly believing in
everything I do.

X

tea
two sugars

Poems of

darkness

love

and the light that comes after.

tea
two sugars

Chapters

The dark

The love

The after light

tea
two sugars

Dark.

tea
two sugars

The sunflower

remains a sunflower

glorious in patience

tall in hope

even on the days

of rain

because she knows

for every day of rain

a day of sun will follow

and when the mother sun arrives

she will send her rays

to shine down upon her face

illuminating the glow

of her yellow.

tea
two sugars

You scream the pain

from your lungs

in silence

but still

i hear you

you are not alone

let me hold your hand

let me walk with you

i will hold you up

i will carry you.

tea
two sugars

There is no goodbye

to a bond

that is deeper

than the deepest

ocean.

There is a lot of good to be said

about the people

who can put on a brave face

get up and face the day

there is also a lot of good to be said

about the people that cannot

you are not less worthy

of life

if your level of capability

to face the world today

is zero.

you are worthy regardless!

tea
two sugars

I do not talk so much

about the death

of my father

anymore

words have become

an injustice to the feeling.

i live in silent battles

tea
two sugars

Nothing in life

                  can prepare you

for missing someone

                  so much

you can be forced

                  to your knees

in surrender

                  on any given day.

tea
two sugars

I spent years wondering

why beauty had abandoned me.

I forgot what i looked like

i forgot what i loved like.

when cancer came for him

my curls uprooted from my scalp

a lot of what remained

turned painfully white

i prayed to god

to keep you safe

every night

it did not work

Wishes

I have always loved

with a whole heart

it is the thing about me

i am most proud of

i told you always

how much i loved

and adored you

even as a child

the words of

i love you

left my lips

as easily as breath

i said i loved you

tea
two sugars

a thousand times

and

i will still die

wishing

i had said it

a thousand and one.

tea
two sugars

On the last morning

the rain came

and then the sun

she called you home

and you went.

I see you

in the eyes

of my brother

but the regret

it ages

his skin

if you

could lay

with him

a while

send whispers

that you

forgive him.

tea
two sugars

Weekly battles with anxiety

Permanent state of flight or fight

teeth clenched

jaw tight.

just relax baby

you're ok

just another monday

After the fall

after the impact

you get to know darkness

on a personal level

it binds itself

to any remaining light

but this darkness

that lays with you

in your bed

is not infinite

this is not where you will live

it is just for now

that this place

this space

tea
two sugars

is a depth

necessary

for you

to transition

from the caterpillar

to the butterfly.

tea

two sugars

i would have fought giants

to keep you

i was lost

after the loss

every day

i tried

to claw my way back

fighting the giants

to keep myself

It is ok
if you have built your walls high
you are worth the protection
but leave the door open
because one day
you will want to walk back through
to meet yourself again.

The aftermath of every heartbreak

tea
two sugars

I had open wounds

that did not stop bleeding.

drip drip

You said you loved
the taste of me

that i was
an exotic fruit
sweet and inviting
from which you just
could not get enough

but it was only ever
in the shadows
late on a Saturday evening
that you craved my body
and your appetite
for my curves
became ravenous enough
to replace all logic
for the both of us

from one Saturday evening
to the next
i let you
bite into me
and take chunks
as you pleased
then i let you
leave a perpetual
trail of confusion
and frustration
for the other
6 days of the week.
Why?/why not?

He did not believe

in another place

after this one

but

if i

am not able

to believe

that he is with me

in some way

then there is no recovery.

finding my way without my father

tea
two sugars

To heal

you must tear yourself apart

and look inside

with an **honest heart.**

tea
two sugars

Desperation surrounded me
it entered through every pore
ripped through my flesh
until i felt the fear
in my bones

yet
with shaking knees
i thrust my hips
off the ground

just a little

and the next day

just a little more

consequently
eventually
the fear turned to dust
came out as faith
and
that is what got
me here.

perseverance
and lots of tea

tea
two sugars

We were born

into two different religions

believing in different things

for different reasons

we would never work

he said *its forbidden*

but when our souls said *hi*

and after midnight

our bodies combined

there was no boundary

anyone could manifest

to keep us apart

but as the night left

so did i.

I lay still in the river
she knows me well
she has taken the agony
from me
a million times before
i let the water wash over me
giving her the permission
to cleanse the torture
from my skin.

she knows exactly
where to touch

tea
two sugars

He said i was beautiful

but how did he know

when he had not

heard me talk

about my passions

and all the things

i cared so deeply

about yet.

-lies

It was easy to love myself

on the good days

but it was loving myself

on the bad days

through the mistakes

i had made

and kept making

through the guilt

and through the shame

that quite frankly

seemed impossible

at times.

tea
two sugars

I pulled the stars down

from the sky

in rage

and begged them

to shine bright

from inside me

so that you could see

that i was so many things

other than pretty.

you did not

I clawed at the ground

dug a hole

amongst the weeds

i buried my heart

along with the seeds

containing every memory

of us together

and covered it with mud

there was no going back

not this time....

most days
i felt it ALL
for all of them

i carried as much
of their weight
on my back
as i could take

i knew it was my duty
as a human
to hold them
and help with the pain
even if it was only
in the smallest of ways

burdens and blessings
of an empath

mostly blessings

tea
two sugars

My heart was not broken

it was torn in half

into two pieces

one piece left in my chest

the other

you took with you

to another side.

i'll never get it back

tea
two sugars

I made promises to myself

i did not keep.

-sorry

tea
two sugars

With feelings

he did not have

he said things

he did not mean

but i liked to listen.

tea
two sugars

When we use hateful language
to speak to ourselves
it enters our veins
like poison
shrinking us
with cruelty
and without forgiveness
until we become numb

it then continues
against our will
to spit off our tongue
and circulate
around our body
so easily
and so freely

that eventually
we become
hardly recognisable
to our own self.

Dark language

tea
two sugars

He said he wanted

to see me naked

so i split open

my chest

and showed him

where i had come from

all that had made me.

the dirty and the clean

tea
two sugars

no going back

when you left this world

i lost all mental clarity

completely shaken at the root

i would never be the same

like i was before

i did not want to be

tea
two sugars

The noise

that left

my lungs

when you left

this earth

was a **THUNDER**

i had never heard

it was the breaking

of my insides.

tea
two sugars

I thought i might drown

in the tears

they were torrential

on the best days

and invisible

on the worst.

tea
two sugars

the flowers

will not bloom

in spring this year

or next

maybe

the flowers

will not

bloom in spring

ever again

without you

.

The moon shone

beautifully bright tonight

exactly like

the night before

as if everything

was the same

i felt betrayed

by her lack of compassion

i never looked at her

in the same way again.

i am destroyed

yet the world keeps turning

tea
two sugars

You left

and so

i do not care

for the sweetness

of peaches

anymore.

-Bitterness

tea
two sugars

The wind

she held my face

reminding me

that i was still here

and i could still feel something.

She came in

through the gaps

in the curtains

i did not want her here

but she insisted

i breathe

feel her warmth

and let my skin

bask in her life.

Sun

tea
two sugars

I was burning

while i was blossoming

there was no peace.

-The art of transitioning

tea
two sugars

When it was time

she beat her drum

it was a familiar sound

we followed

because her life

depended on it

as did ours

i stood

side by side

with my sisters

i knew their traumas

and they knew mine.

Binding experiences

tea
two sugars

i sat with

what was broke

it was a reminder

i was still alive

not yet ready to die

Another starting again

she tried to hide
the destruction
that had remained
from past wars
but too often
it demanded to be seen

so
she practised
talking with soft words
and gentle tones
first to herself
and then
to him

she hoped
she did not
destroy it
before it began.

tea
two sugars

Buried traumas

there are special places
on the inside of me
with cracks so deep
not even the sun
can get in
to shine its light there.

tea
two sugars

he was scared to leave

not having the chance

to say yes

to so many of the things

he had once said no to

no more chances

no more choices

only this moment

only now

The resilient heart

My heart has ruptured

many times

pain has seeped through

into my soul

for different reasons

for different people

but the heart

is made

to carry

every emotion

at every magnitude

and the heart

will heal

almost entirely

tea
two sugars

with love and patience

some scars may remain

perhaps for a lifetime

but the heart will beat

and it will be strong

finding new purposes

to stay alive.

tea
two sugars

Forehead on the bathroom floor

NO STRENGTH LEFT

NOTHING

NOTHING

NOTHING

almost nothing.

Depression- a new battle

Sometimes when my thoughts
are dark
my mind splits open in fury
and bursts into flames
it scatters the pieces
of what i know
of how i cope
far and wide
without mercy

sometimes the darkness stays
and consumes me entirely
forcing me
to seek solace
in silent places
and just be nothing

i wait
desperately hoping
to be rescued

people come
of course
and they try
but they hardly ever
break in

so i surrender
and i am quiet
for a while
out of acknowledgment
out of respect

knowing
there is no other way out
nothing else to be done
but to let the darkness
pass through me
and then when it is time
i will move my feet
and carry myself out

kissing myself
for surviving its wrath.

Your eyes

give away

your cruel intentions

but the words

that fall from your mouth

are warm

and inviting

and just like yesterday

they caress my wrists

and ankles

into position.

Restriction through manipulation

tea
two sugars

When you lose

the person

you love

the most

you never

move on

you just spend

your days

looking for ways

to convince your heart

to keep beating.

it's exhausting

tea
two sugars

He took me impolitely

my bruised body

opened

without resistance

and let in

the 6th time

second chance

my heart did not.

tea
two sugars

There have been many times

i have needed space

to love myself privately

there have been many times

i have needed space

to hate myself privately

either way

do not disturb.

tea
two sugars

He chose her

and i chose

to justly

punish my body

for not providing you

with the home

you needed

like she has.

tea
two sugars

There are thoughts

i have thought

of myself

to myself

so hateful

and

so hurtful

they have left marks

on my skin

it was a painful truth

to acknowledge

that i have spent my lifetime

abusing myself

from within.

tea
two sugars

Grief

this lesson
is one
i do not want
i cannot find
the blessing
in this

i cannot
even do it
for my daughter
today
like they so often
sympathetically insist

because the feelings of despair
do not go away
just looking at her face.

oh god i wish they did

tea
two sugars

i will rest

and without the strength

i will do it all again

tomorrow

I had never
seen its face
before
i had only
heard tales

i had been living
without
any real regard
for its existence

until now

on this morning
it showed itself
to me

it stood
right in front of me
like an old friend
i had forgotten

it covered
my most loved one
like a shield
of finality and mercy

i asked death
to allow me one
more glimpse
of my dad

as i had known him

NO
how selfish you are
to ask
when life
has given you
so much more
than one glimpse

on this morning
i was forced
to see
life and death
as one in the same

never one
without the other
existing
in perfect compliment
to one another
the beginning and the end
the end and the beginning

i left that day
both dead and alive

i both feared
and anticipated its arrival
for myself.

tea
two sugars

Love.

for me
there is no greater experience
in this world
than to be loved
and to love
to such an unbelievably
overwhelming extent
that you are
both
lifted
and broken
from the same feeling

how very worth it
it all was
for my heart
to have been so alive
in your company

how very worth it
you were
my love

i would choose it all again

tea
two sugars

Learning to love yourself

is hugging

with careful hands

from the inside out.

.

Forgiveness

i ask for forgiveness
for the ways
i am yet
to punish myself
i will learn to do better

be with yourself

on this day

and every day after

in unconditional forgiveness.

(you will need it)

Your body is your home

it holds all your secrets

and all your stories

this is the first place

you must fall in love

and the last.

Aphrodite give me guidance

hands placed

for pleasure

no resistance

she evoked

her inner

sleeping goddess

and remained present

allowing her chest

to feel her breath

fire energy

radiated

just underneath

her skin

water energy

tea
two sugars

began to flow

separate to the blood

in her veins.

so this is what

it feels like

to be all awake

no shame

tea
two sugars

it is love

and only love

that stands in the way

of the complete destruction

of everything alive on this planet

tea
two sugars

I found healing

in every moment

i drank tea

with my best friend.

tea
two sugars

Be gentle with yourself
your everything you have.

Be kind with yourself
your everything you have.

Be patient with yourself
your everything you have.

tea
two sugars

She was proud

of the wrinkles on her cheeks

and the dark under her eyes

because behind them

there was a tale

a heartbreak

a triumph

a loss

some to be told

some to be kept.

tea
two sugars

He took off my clothes

and looked at me

like he was looking

at heaven

lights on

face up

let my body glow

diamonds on my head

i wear myself well.

i am secure with my insecurities

tea
two sugars

I took
my mind
to hell
trying to guess
what he thought
about me

i took
my body
to hell
trying to sculpt it
into the perfect
shape
to appeal
to the tastes
i thought he had

i did not manage it
it did not exist

*i apologise
to myself
for the abuse*

i love you.

tea
two sugars

Life is

all the joys

and

all the sorrows

all the pain

and

all the glory.

tea
two sugars

You will fly

or i will catch you.

tea
two sugars

Being a mother

is heaven.

and

a little bit

soul destroying

The honesties of motherhood

i will try and heal you

with my words

i will hug you

until it no longer hurts

but you will still feel it all

open up

let it in

these pains

and these pleasures

are the making of you

this will be the story

you will tell

Raising Asia

tea
two sugars

It was winter

but your shine

was summer

velvet skin

every inch of you

is gold

you grew the confidence

to love

the way your body

holds.

tea
two sugars

When you love yourself

as a requirement

there will not be a need

for any more explanations

to anyone

not to him

not to her

not even to yourself.

tea
two sugars

cry

i will stay

(the beauty in vulnerability)

Better the tears flow out
than remain and build a river within.

Cry to people
let people cry to you.

tea

two sugars

Taking care of yourself

is knowing there will be bad days

but you will hold yourself tight

and love yourself through it.

Unconditional love of ourselves

tea
two sugars

Home

I have never found my home

in a place

i love many places

but they do not love me back

my home

she is in the hearts and holds

of my people

settled over near and distant lands.

i liked the way

my skin

hugged my bones

for bigger

for smaller

i was with her

until death parted us

(thankyou body for carrying me)

tea
two sugars

I had to retrain my mind

to look at my body

in a different way

instead of with disgust and comparison

with pride and gratitude

i started telling it

every day

the abundance of things

i loved most about it

instead of

every little thing

i most hated.

tea
two sugars

i have admittedly fallen

for

words

laced with honey

more times than i care to count

(i like that sweet talk)

we sat with each other
in candle light
cross legged
vulnerable
we shared our stories
with quiet voices
in their most
honest versions

it wasn't roses

it was raw
it was depth
it was a sharing of pain
a vibrational exchange
based on mutual love and freedom

and after
when we no longer needed words

the frequency of the vibe
remained high
authentic moments of

oh i see you boo
hi

tea
two sugars

I prayed on a thousand

cold nights

to bring me a love

that would make the rose buds

open

and show their pretty faces

early this year.

tea
two sugars

I sometimes wonder

if i enjoy the pain

because honestly

i just did not want it

if it did not almost

destroy me

i fear living

without ever

having my heart broken

again.

Love stories

They have loved me

off the ledge

every single time

my heart beats

for

unconditional friendships.

tea
two sugars

i will let you see

the darkness first

that is the type

of love

i want

tea
two sugars

nice to see you again

I am certain

our souls

knew each other

in previous lives

long before

we met

in this one

and that is why

loving you is so easy

i knew it was you

and you knew it was me.

tea
two sugars

I would paint your picture

but the colours for you

don't exist yet.

Beauty beyond comprehension

Beautiful black baby

The sun lives in the darkness

of your melanin

a perfect contrast

to the light within

your hair

is as intended

growing gloriously

towards the heavens

a reminder

of where you came from.

tea
two sugars

You must

love your self

harder

after

all of them

have left.

The ground

never even looked the same

after he walked on it

daffodils grew

out of the concrete.

<u>Extraordinary dad</u>

I imagine one day
to make love
and i will know it is love
because you will ask me
to share with you
my desires

and in confidence
i will tell you
i will show myself to you
without fear

you will take care
with me
when you enter
taking your time

making the kisses
long and lasting

seeing me in my moment
before you have yours.

I will not stand by

and let them decide

anything of who i am

or will be

i am perfectly capable

of convincing myself

i am worth something

or not

I AM.

My body is my temple

sacred ground

it is mine

and mine alone

i will decide

how it lives

who comes in

and what stays (energies included).

Love has asked me

many times

to not be

so careless with it

but i have never learned

quite frankly

i never hope to

mainly because

i am not convinced

that there is any beauty

to be found

in a life

so cautious of risk.

tea
two sugars

I learned to

speak

to myself

in truths

those that filled me

and the those that

left me

completely empty

both were equally

as necessary.

tea
two sugars

I will make it

my life's work

to worship

all the parts

of you

that

you do not adore

because i see who you are

and i am here

for all of you.

tea
two sugars

The hundreds and hundreds
of minutes
you have spent
hoping
to be
just like her
have floated away
evaporated into the air

gone
not to be given back

and *you* are still
wonderfully
just like *you*
and will remain
perfectly
just as *you*
for your time here
on this earth
you must get right with that
because *you* darling
are as magnificent
as *you* get.

We were in college
i knew nothing
for certain
other than
he was magic
and i
was spellbound.

(teenage love affairs that change the way we see the world)

tea
two sugars

Create yourself

in your own image

grow nicely into your shape

and into your mind

you will be grateful to yourself

forever for it.

.

His hands

caressed my thighs

with such tenderness

handling their parting

with gentle fingers

he knew that i was a treasure

and inside was where

the gold was hidden.

tea
two sugars

He said hi

and asked my name

i gave him my heart

in a box

and wrote fragile

on the front.

(*please take care*)

fragile

handle with care

I was a broken woman

yet life

was still full

of so much beautiful

i could not help

but fall in love

with life again

watching the way

the sun said goodnight

in bali.

Maybe
you
like me
have spent
copious amounts
of time
looking
on the outside
of yourself
for love.

Waiting
to meet love
waiting
for love
to be spoken
into the air
for your ears
to hear
waiting
for love
to enter
your body
and make you
feel whole.

But too often
it has
arrived as glitter
and left
as dust
and you

again
are questioning
whether love
knows
where you live
almost
entirely convinced
you have been
missed
from
the
deserving of the one
list.

But there of course
is no such list
and you
most certainly
have not
been missed.

Because true love
lives within
it is in
the ground
of you
where your feet
stand
and in
the heavens
of you
where your head rests.

Only with this acceptance
can love
fall into you
and then after
expand
out
from your
finger tips
into
the fingertips
of other loves.

And even
if along
the way
the seeds
you have planted
become unearthed
and the threads
you have sewn
are twisted
and pulled
that love will
not be broken
it will remain
truer
than true
because
the truest love
begins unconditionally
on the inside of you.

tea
two sugars

The After
Light.

tea
two sugars

I inhaled the smoke

of every single fire

i lit

and allowed it

to burn my chest.

as a reminder

of my failures

and of my victories

The truth of who you are

lies in the conversations

you have with yourself

when the lights go out

and the world is sleeping.

tea
two sugars

Her beautiful

came from

behind the eyes

her beautiful

was a connection

to the world

without wifi.

Substance for the win

You must decide
that you are a glorious being
with glorious gifts
and that you will not
live from a place of conformity
where even your heart
forgets the magic
that belongs
uniquely to you

it will be the greatest injustice
to yourself
and your journey on this earth
if you do not let
your inside *being* burn
in its purpose

for what else is there...

tea
two sugars

Here you are

you crawled out
of that place
where death resides

you did not think
you could do it
but *here you are*

despite the adversities
that should have destroyed
here you are

with courage
and
complete
commitment
to yourself
that
there are **no**
no's
for you
when you came back
from death.

Guidance

It was when i shut my eyes

and i was lost

in between places

that the words poured out of my mind.

a gift from the other side

There will come a day

where all you have survived

will make sense

it will mean something

it will heal something

but before that

there will be many days

where all you have survived

will make no sense at all.

the bad before the good

the good before the great

it is an unavoidable process

your evolution will not be pretty

We are as strong
as they think we are

Revolution pending.

tea
two sugars

The presentation

of constant perfection

for their viewing

will break your mind

some days

fuck it.

tea
two sugars

I fold the corners

of my favourite pages

in every book i read

so i know where to get help

in emergency situations.

Let your body shine in the light

nourish it

with kind words

and kisses

run your fingers

over every stretchmark

and every scar

over the precious parts

that are darker

through every area

covered in hair

let all that has made you

feel insecure

bend towards the sun

with more than acceptance

with honour and freedom.

We have

crawled

walked

skipped

ran

and sometimes

been dragged

down the same paths

so

we know the same secrets

my girls and i

i am with her

because i am her

here to empower

and be empowered.

Women for Women

Life goals

I hope
in my final days
my skin and mind
have aged
perfectly ripe
without regret

i hope
in my final hours
to wear a smile
luminous and proud
knowing my heart and soul
have lived bright
like a starry night sky
in november
because they chose a life
of happiness
of passion
of purpose

i hope
in my last moments
as i take my final breath
my eyes close
with courage
and my hearing fades
to the final sounds
of a life time's worth
of adventures.

tea
two sugars

Your intuition

is your greatest power

it does not lie

it is whispers and teachings

of every lesson

passed on

from every woman

it is the richest knowledge

from the mothers

who have gone

from this land

it knows all things

let it speak

listen

in its guidance

you will not fail.

tea
two sugars

I am empowered

from the things

i have lived through

that have not

put an end to me.

tea
two sugars

Sometimes we are women

who drink tea

and talk about

past heartbreaks

and future plans

sometimes we are girls

who drink spiced rum

in back gardens

and do not go home.

Humans

They tear pieces off the earth
and demand
you do not cross
they switch your narrative
and make it ugly

but the human in us
sees the human in you
your journey
is the ultimate account
of courage

you will never be illegal
in a world
that is yours
as much as it is theirs.

we (all of us)
come from
the same
divine mother

tea
two sugars

The sight of her brown skin

covered in shea butter

and nothing else

was mesmerising

she was a divine being.

she will make

salt taste sweet

if you let her

tea
two sugars

The ones who can

will speak

with sharp tongues

without mercy

for the ones who can't.

tea
two sugars

There is no comfort in these words for you

i am not here with nurturing intentions

just **the truths** of the battles

with words as my weapon.

tea
two sugars

I will give my daughter

wings and a voice

so that she is able

to fly free from all restraints

and speak from a place

truly belonging

only to her

i will teach my daughter

to worship

her whole beautiful self

everything in

and everything out

as it is there

she will find meaning

it is there

she will find god.

Life's work

Make it your life's work

to discover

and then rediscover

who you are

otherwise

others will do it for you

and you might believe them.

The poem was her

everything she was

and

everything she wasn't.

<u>Perfection</u>

The freeness

my mother has given me

in letting me be who i am

in any

and every way i choose

without judgement

has privileged me

to live a life

as myself

that i am not afraid of.

what a gift

tea
two sugars

With a beautiful heart

and a beautiful mind

you will be seen

and you will be heard.

i write everything

i have seen and heard

from the back

and the front

everything

that has torn through my skin

and theirs

i write our experiences

and share them with you

so you know

you are not alone

tea
two sugars

It wasn't until

i wrote down the words

of all the things

i was afraid to say out loud

that i was free.

tea
two sugars

Green tea
no honey
and stories
of every orgasm
i didn't have.

They said it was the way of things

a man's place

a woman's place

but i knew i was a *wild thing*

and my appetite for wildness

did not allow

for any particular way of things

other than my own.

even if i did not

always know the direction

my failings

are no coincidence

i believe them

to have been perfectly placed

by god herself

to draw out

the darkness

and the light

uncovering

the most honest parts

of myself

so when i am asked

who i am

i will certainly know

tea
two sugars

look past the bones

that steady us

for this experience

see behind the lines

of difference

listen to people

who do not

look like you

it will rip you open

when you realise

we have connections

with each other

that go beyond

our bodies

(show compassion to your fellow human)

tea
two sugars

I let my clothes

fall off

then i danced

with myself

to words

from songs

that understood

what i had been through.

music will help to heal you

tea
two sugars

The truth is

we spend most of our lives

in perpetual growth

under construction

half way between a sunrise

and a sunset.

I am interested in the stories

of those

who use an art

to escape

and live beyond the

realities of this world.

tea
two sugars

My roots fall deep

into the ground

strong

and

coiled

and like the trees

who stand firm

around me

i was made to outlast

every storm.

Book shops

will remind you

that you were

once a child

with the craziest

of dreams

that were unequivocally possible

to achieve

without ever even

concerning yourself

with how

it will be done.

You cannot know
how it will work out

we are dying
trying to control futures
that have not happened
yet

you can plan
you can prepare
but please do not
torment yourself
trying to figure out
how exactly
it will manifest

(because this part has nothing to do with you)

be present
work on the now
speak it to the universe
trust
open up
surrender

it will come to pass
when it will come to pass.

let go baby

Everything changes

in the name of growth

it must

there is no glory

in standing still

for longer than is necessary

(necessary being individually subjective)

the old practises must die.

tea
two sugars

Fresh mint tea
in a coffee shop
waiting for the world
to notice me.

tea
two sugars

you look like heaven

purely as yourself

tea
two sugars

She was already half way

up the mountain

    lifted from the sacrifices (told and untold)

      of those who had walked before

                she grew her wings

                  on the way

               and what a marvel

                  she became.

Darling

you could

long before

you told yourself

you couldn't

there is magic

in your art

in your voice

in your words

there is magic

in your eyes

in your strength

in your heart.

tea
two sugars

I will love you so much

it will flow out of you

then you will have no choice

but to love yourself

in the very same way.

tea
two sugars

You need to stop

for more than a second

much more

than once in a while

otherwise

you might miss

the whole thing.

Yours sincerely

life

tea
two sugars

There is something about growing up

that can destroy us

regaining the sight

of our childhood eyes

is the enlightenment.

tea
two sugars

It was everything

and then it was nothing.

just lust passing through
just lust passing through
just lust passing through
just lust passing through
just lust passing through
just lust passing through

tea
two sugars

You may need something

stronger than tea.

(Rare catch ups)

I give a piece of myself

to everyone i meet

and every time i do

i wonder

if one day

there will be no more pieces of me

left to give

and i will just disappear.

but what a glorious disappearance that would be

tea
two sugars

I jumped in

head first

heart first

there was no time to catch my breath.

(new romances)

tea
two sugars

Resist their labels

do not let them stick to you

as well as

any socially constructed ideas

of what is possible

there is no limit

to what you can do

unless of course

you believe that there is.

The telling of your experiences
will encourage bravery
into a thousand hearts.

tea
two sugars

The darkness and light in you

are bound together

you must make space for both.

(Balance)

tea
two sugars

Perspective

he told me

i was crazy

i told him

i was passion

the right mix

of chaos and art

righteously living.

You may feel like today
has been a day
in which
you have been pushed
way beyond
any point of return

blood stains on your hands
broken
beaten
bruised

the world
is simply not the place
you remember it to be

but *i know you*
and i know that you can rebuild
from the fragments
that have come undone

i have witnessed you
in battle before
and every day
when the day begins again
so can you.

hold on
always one more day

tea
two sugars

All the parts of you

that you have concealed

show them to me

so that you can heal.

^

tea
two sugars

I don't know about tomorrow
but today is not the day
i give in.

good morning

tea
two sugars

I believe it

to be true

that

the stars

illuminating the sky

are the forgotten dreams

of millions of people

who have not used them

to illuminate their lives.

-reminders of all that is still possible

tea
two sugars

We will show you outrageous

we will break open in flames

when you try to break us.

-The oppressed

From the moment you uncover

and authentically declare

yourself

as you are

the entire universe

will move to your music

it will be the most vulnerable

yet the most sincere

you will ever be.

You looked closely

at the brutality

of my grey parts

and offered me a closer look

at yours

then we collided

i celebrated your universe

and you celebrated mine

there was no need

for anything else

i was me

and you were you.

Reciprocation

tea
two sugars

<u>Motherhood</u>

I will follow you

across any galaxy

because we were destined

to travel together

ever since

our energies combined

and you grew from the outside of me.

tea
two sugars

I smiled
day
after
day

and said nothing

yet
i so desperately hoped
this time
my eyes
would give away
the conflict inside

and somebody would notice.

help

Tears are my hearts voice
her sadness
her joy
a show of her pain

they are death
anger
transition
growth
reflection
love

sometimes they come out
in floods
and surround the ground
where i lay
nourishing and enriching
past traumas
that have been purposefully starved
and buried
in order for me
to stay alive

traumas that now
choose to surface
and hold space
for a time
so that i may close the wound.

tea
two sugars

Ask me questions

that make me wriggle in my seat

in discomfort.

getting to know each other

after the small talk

he was smooth
like 90's rnb

i moved to his beat
so willingly

my hips swayed
into his rhythm

he stroked
my hair
and my body
and my spirit

i began
to forget
the list of things
i had told
myself
i would not do
tonight

i guess
i will live for the moment tonight
and be mad at myself tomorrow

tea
two sugars

The words have not been

put together

for the poem

to describe your light

and how your first breath

saved my life.

My aura has felt

the weight

of my stress lately

these pressures

have carved lines

into my face faintly

i asked the mother for help

she told me

to look

to the earth

for the remedy.

We have pretty strong thighs

passed down from our mothers

generations have passed

and we are tired

of holding them all

on our shoulders

we are the bearers of pain

the physical and the mental

we wear the crown

but so often

it leans heavy

on our temples.

The expectations of womanhood

tea
two sugars

Sometimes

i do not say what i mean

occasionally

i struggle to express

how i feel

yet

i still let the words leave

and escape into empty spaces.

maybe i will use them later

tea
two sugars

Love does not hurt

un loves hurts

un truths hurt

broken promises hurt

love does not hurt

love is the thing

on the other side

of all that hurts

and destroys

you have known pain

and because of that

you will know love.

stay open

tea
two sugars

How to say goodbye?

there isn't a way

but i will continue

to pray

for us to meet again

for another hello.

tea
two sugars

You must live

with a willing heart

a heart that dies

and comes back to life

time and again

we must accept that this

is the process of life

dying and living

dying and living

there is no hiding from it

and

it is our participation

resilience

patience

tea
two sugars

and willingness

towards this process

time and again

that determines

how full the life is

we live.

There is a full

galaxy beneath

would you care to take a look?

i will show you mine

if you show me yours.

(more than faces and bodies)

tea
two sugars

Life can make us hard

cover us in spikes

but oh my

isn't it also

so lovely

because i am certain

that there is nothing

more worth it

than the two of us

standing here

together

in love

in this moment

on this afternoon.

tea
two sugars

my love

Under no circumstance

do you let any words

from any mouth

in any tone

convince you that you

do not have greatness in you.

We will not shrink ourselves. We will not shrink
ourselves. We will not shrink ourselves.

tea
two sugars

gods

give power

to the galaxies

that live in our hands

let our words

expand

and collide

with the hearts

of those

who do not

know peace

let the collision

be enough

to unsettle

the sands

on their graves

enough

to ignite

a fire

in their blood

with equal measures

of rage

and love

let them

rise

and redeem

the destroyed

only then

shall we be worthy

to welcome death

when it comes for us

tea
two sugars

(many stories have been told)

I have heard so much

told so much

felt so much

and learnt so much

over tea

that started

with two sugars.

tea
two sugars

Printed in Poland
by Amazon Fulfillment
Poland Sp. z o.o., Wrocław

53383840R00112